Thinking Out Loud

Poems from the Heart

Arlene Baptiste

AuthorHouse™ UK Ltd.
500 Avebury Boulevard
Central Milton Keynes, MK9 2BE
www.authorhouse.co.uk
Phone: 08001974150

© *2009 Arlene Baptiste. All rights reserved.*

No part of this book may be reproduced, stored in a retrieval system, or transmitted by any means without the written permission of the author.

First published by AuthorHouse 10/1/2009

ISBN: 978-1-4490-2094-1 (sc)

This book is printed on acid-free paper.

This book is dedicated to God, my family and friends

Contents

The Flame of Youth	1
Back to God	2
Talents	3
Temper	4
Fault Finders	5
Judges	6
A Friend	7
Love	8
A Diamond	9
Where Am I Going?	10
Cloudy Days	11
Treasured Daughter	12
The Walk	13
Talking to God	14
My Prayer	15
Mr Right	16
Keeping Hope Alive	17
Wisdom for a Husband	18
The Rocky Road	19
Beautiful Thoughts	20
Memories	21
1 Corinthians 13	22
God's Perfect Will	23
Bountiful are Gods Blessings	24
Recognise	26
Value in Christ	27

Consider	29
Getting Older	30
Positivity	31
Death	32
A Winter's Night	33
About the Author	34

The Flame of Youth

Struck ablaze and illuminating
Consuming darkness, in all your glory
In gentle breeze, you flicker in your nakedness
Ever bright, and glowing.

You're tossed and blown
From one course to another
Dancing in the winds of change
Hot with life, and with living.

You have choices:
Illuminate, bring warmth or destroy.
You hold the power;
Keep on burning
Let none put you out.
And may God direct your flame always.

Back to God

My faith was low and I was young,
I thought that I knew more
Than what was taught to me of God
But of course I wasn't sure.
I searched for understanding
From words of mortal men
But still they gave no answers to
The search there was within.
But never did I once dismiss
The thought that God was there
And after I discovered that
My burdens he did bear.
Now my heart is filled with joy
There's no emptiness inside
For I've found a loving Saviour
Who's my strength, my hope and guide.

Talents

To each and every one it's true
The Lord has placed a talent or two.
He wants us to discover all -
No matter whether great or small.
What you need to know is that
Those things which we are gifted at
Pay off no doubt, so persevere -
The key is you must conquer fear.

Temper

A soft word said with tempers calm
Will not provoke and cause great harm.
What gain is there to rage and shout?
That's not what Christian life's about.

Endorsing peace should be our goal,
To firmly keep our self control
What's needed is a change of heart
So let us make that vital start.

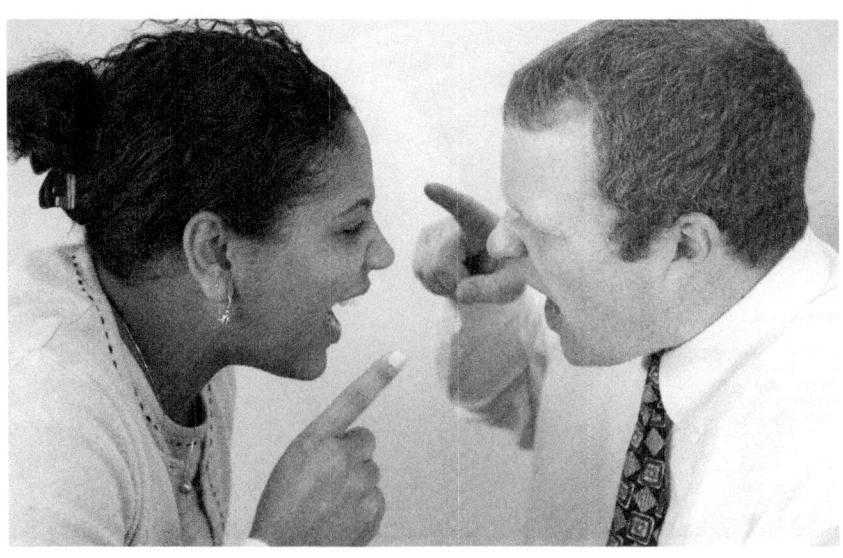

Fault Finders

Your outlook's all wrong, your ignorance blinding
You cannot control your constant fault finding.
When out comes the sun, you'll complain it won't last,
And all you will see is the shadows it casts.
The sun shines with bright and beautiful rays
That benefit earth, in so many ways.
Be bright, be happy, be hopeful, be free,
For this is the outlook I wish you could see.

Judges

Set lifestyle, one mindset, so ridged won't budge
Causing repression, folks fear to be judged.
Freedom and expression cannot show their head
Life without choices, or voices, is dead.

Christ Jesus, our Saviour, is whom we must trust.-
Providing we choose him, the rest's down to us.
Our journey is personal, and very unique,
Lord Jesus, you're worthy alone to critique.

A Friend

Where can I find a friend so true?
For such as those are seldom few
To lend an ear and hear my cry
And comfort bring as time goes by,

To cheer me up when I am low
Encourage hope to spiritually grow.
A cheerful smile, a warm embrace
Can brighten up the dullest face.

I hope that I can also be
Someone who hears another's plea.
A caring heart is what I'll lend
And only hope I was a friend.

Love

Love is a balm that soothes the heart,
That moves the very deepest part,
A resounding joy inside your soul
That leaves me feeling strangely whole.

I feel love in different ways:
Through kindly words and Godly praise,
Through cheerful smiles and loving deeds,
Love is what everybody needs.

A Diamond

Where can I find that diamond?
I saw it one day in the sun,
I picked it up from off of the ground
And thought that it was the one.
I polished it up and I treasured it,
Thinking that it was so rare.
I didn't want to lose it
So I held it with love and with care,
But as I looked down I noticed
Some blood seeping from my sore hand
For the diamond had cut deep within me
And now wasn't looking so grand.
For in fact when the sun had ceased shining
What I discovered that day in the grass
Is the diamond I held and I treasured
Was a broken old piece of cheap glass!
Oh where can I find that diamond?
The one that is priceless and rare
In a world full of cubic zirconiums
Is there one last diamond to spare?

Where Am I Going?

Where am I going on this journey called life?
I wish I was sheltered from heartache and strife.
God gave me life, and my mum gave me birth
But what is my purpose, my reason on earth?

If I am loved, will it ever be felt?
A heart that is frozen, can it ever melt?
If there's a key that can unlock one's heart
Will mine be jammed? Will it fall apart?

A heart that is human is subject to pain
Surely needs shelter from a battering rain.
I'll keep mine protected, and seal it up tight
Till God in his wisdom, reveals Mr Right.

Cloudy Days

Beneath a cloud is where I lay
It follows me from day to day.
I stare into the stormy sky
And hope that it would pass me by,
But rain still beats upon my heart -
I feel my world is torn apart.
From yonder breaks a ray of light
That shines with warmth so golden bright.
Now I've no need to feel alone,
For faith and hope in God is known
And clouds above won't seem so dim
Once I've placed my trust in him.

Treasured Daughter

Lord what is your will for me?
Can you hear my heart screaming?
What is my life to be?
Is there nothing worth gleaning?

I am running low Lord, and fast approaching empty -
Don't let me go Lord, for what I need is plenty.
Fill me up Lord, to the brink and overflow,
Give me strength Lord, and plant me where I can grow.

Hold me tight Lord, within your arms of love.
Let me know Lord, you're watching from above.
Let me live Lord, by streams of living water,
Let me be, Lord, your special treasured daughter.

The Walk

Walked desert lands and parched terrain
Can feel the pressure, heat and pain.
My feet are sore, my head is faint,
The land my drops of blood will paint,
And time does not exist no more.
As shadows loom about the floor,
Birds descend to catch their prey.
I will pray, but in a different way -
On bended knees to God I cry
Whilst staring at the scorching sky
Lord break these chains and set me loose
Untie me from this choking noose,
Show me the land where I belong
To walk there bravely, proud and strong
And let me live where waters flow
Beneath my feet where I can grow
And with this water I will pour
Into my mouth and thirst no more.
Please take my hand and walk with me
And lead me onto victory.

Talking to God

Am I talking to God, or just merely thin air?
Like a breeze I can't see Him, but believe that He's there.
Heavenly Father please guide me in all that I do
For it's not very easy, when I don't have a clue.

I'm feeling quite weak, and my future's unknown.
I feel quite discouraged, and totally alone.
God says these are feelings, and feelings don't last
And soon they'll become just a thing of the past.

So I'll keep on believing, and try not to slack
For its comfort to know that my God's got my back.
Gladly I'll follow, wherever he leads,
For He knows my sorrow and all of my needs.

My Prayer

Give me a great future and fill it with joy,
Prevent any circumstances that may destroy
The plans that you have to give me a good life
And one day become a lucky man's wife.

I ask for your favour, and know it is done
Through the power and might, of your begotten son.
Lord, give me your wisdom and insight to see
Any pitfalls that lay straight ahead of me.

Grant me protection, and encompass my home,
And pour out your love, so I don't feel alone.
Thank you, oh Lord, for people who care
And the love that I have inside me to share.

I long to see places that I've never been,
To marvel at beauty I'm yet to have seen
Acknowledging just how awesome you are
As my Lord and my Saviour, and Mighty Creator.

Mr Right

The day I look into his eyes
I'm to withhold no false disguise
But be entranced by such a face
So full of loving, gentle grace.

He'll be patient, kind and modest too
For men like those are seldom few.
Where can I find a man as he?
Believe me, it's a mystery.

From day to day he'll make me smile,
To be with him is well worth while,
And as we journey on through life
I'll know I'm blessed to be his wife.

Well God, my life is in your hands.
From round the corner or across the lands
Where is this man to call my own?
'Cause I don't want to be alone.

Keeping Hope Alive

Whilst I walk through my doorway
Finding nobody to greet,
My heart yearns for and I pray for
A good man to one day meet,
Asking, "How has your day been?"
And if I answer "It was tough."
He'd put his loving arms around me
Saying, "Don't worry 'bout all that stuff."

Oh! One day to enjoy
Sweet and open honesty,
To communicate my thoughts
And feel accepted being me.
It would only be ourselves
On this planet made for two,
There would be nobody else
That could love me like you do.

As we stand the test of time
I'll know that we'd have succeeded
When we know each other's hearts,
With spoken words no longer needed,
For we'd have reached a certain state
A plain, unquestionably known
Where no one could penetrate
Our nurtured love now fully grown.

Wisdom for a Husband

You have a darling wife
Now that you've tied the knot,
Make sure you love her dearly
And with everything you've got.
When you look into her eyes
And feel the tenderness so strong,
It means you've realized
You've found a heart where you belong.

Now there's someone special
To share your hopes, your dreams and fears,
Someone who can hold you
And help wipe away your tears,
Someone who will support you
In those times you're feeling sad,
And will always be there
During good times and the bad.

So live your lives forever
Filled with happiness and fun,
Making choices together,
No longer two, but being one.
Take your time to listen
To understand each other's needs,
And let your home be filled with
Loving words and kindly deeds.

The Rocky Road

God grant me your wisdom with each passing day
As I fall on my knees, and earnestly pray
That your will be done in all that I do
So I walk in your ways and cling dearly to you.

Life's road it is rocky, with multiple tracks
And burdens are heavy inside my rucksack.
I'll keep persevering, and follow your route
Prepared in advance, in your manual of truth.

Though others may mock me, and say I'm insane
To follow an ancient and outdated plane,
As onwards I walk, your plan becomes clear,
Revealing your purpose, and why I am here.

Where this journey ends remains to be known,
But oh how I've learned, experienced and grown.
I look back at my footprints, just where I once trod
And thankful I am you were there with me God.

Beautiful Thoughts

Beautiful thoughts, may they never shatter,
To ignorant folks, feelings don't matter.
From outward appearance, you uphold your pride,
Disguising your pain and your suffering inside.

Be true to your heart, hold onto your dreams,
For they are the lights that turn into sunbeams.
Invest in those things that will make your soul smile
And watch as your life will prove much more worthwhile.

Memories

Reflecting on the days of old,
For memories kept, they are as gold;
And in our hearts is where they stay,
Of which, no one can take away.

The fun we had in times of past -
Wish days like those were made to last;
Hey I'm still young for goodness sake,
I've plenty memories still to make!

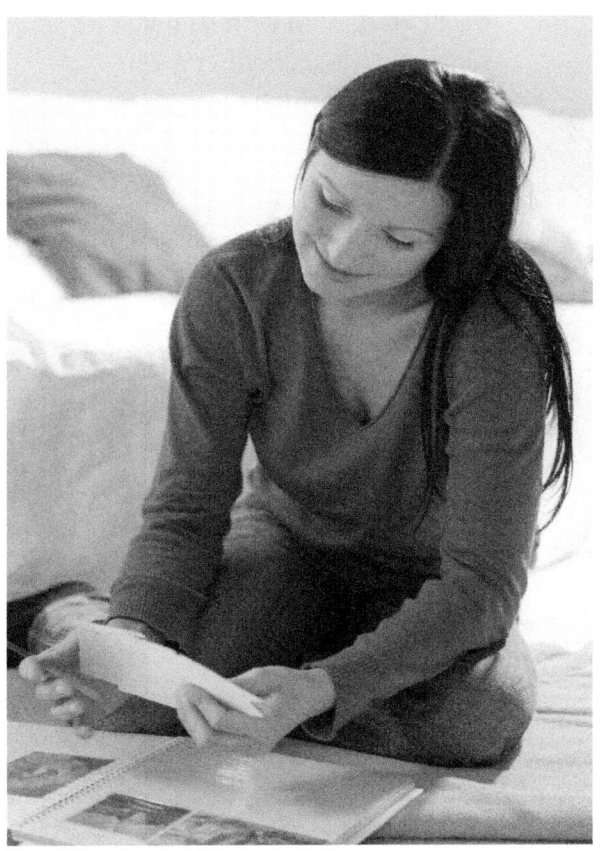

1 Corinthians 13

It is so vital and important
To love God and each other,
Love your neighbour as yourself -
They are your sister and your brother.
Show them patience and kindness,
That is genuine and true
For surely that is what
You'd want them to show to you.
Don't keep bitterness inside,
Or be puffed up with so much pride,
Don't be selfish, neither mean,
Read 1 Corinthians 13.

God's Perfect Will

To do My perfect will are you faithful and able,
Or is your Christianity nothing but a label?
Would you help someone in need, or do a selfless deed?
When trials comes your way, would you always let Me lead?

It's not enough to say you love Me
It's not enough to say you care
It's not enough to say you'll be by My side, when you're not there.
You say you're doing all that's right – that you're walking in My light,
Your actions tell Me more than your words.

Bountiful are Gods Blessings

Bountiful are God's blessings,
His love for me is great,
He's teaching me some lessons
That, thank God, are not too late.

He knows my every sorrow
And feels my every pain.
Yesterday, today, tomorrow
His love is still the same.

He can see just where I am
And where I want to be,
He said to trust in him,
And has plans in place for me.

And as a child needs guiding
I let him take my hand,
For I know that I'm abiding
In rock, not sinking sand.

To those who do not realize
God's power that transforms,
Just open up your hearts eyes
And see, he's been there all along.

For he sent a risen Saviour
Whose arms are open wide,
He will always love you
And not judge or criticize.

But to him give all the glory
And praise his holy name,
Then your life, which is a story
It will never be the same.

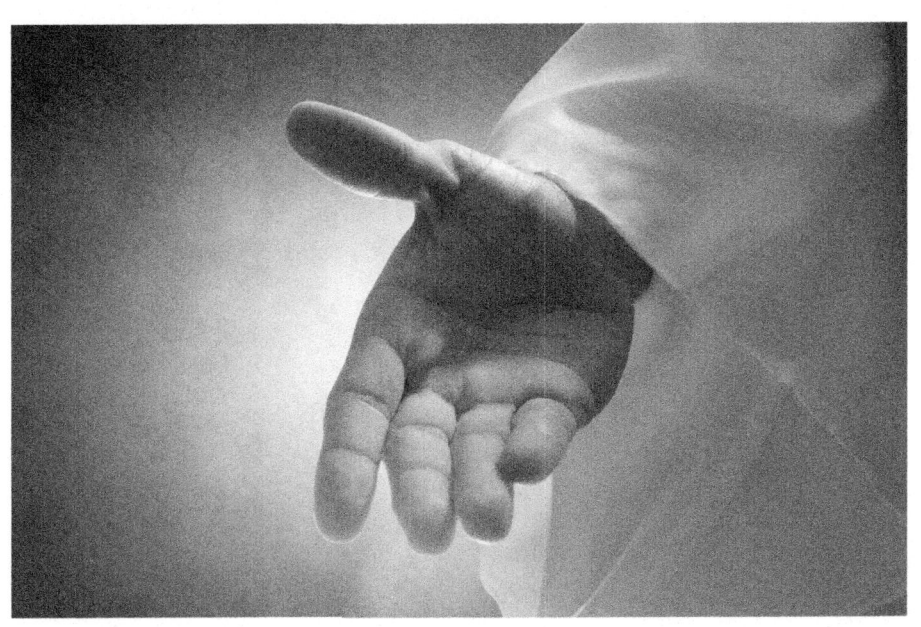

Recognise

Recognise all my talents, recognise that I'm good,
I long to be someday totally understood
As the person I am, the one that is me -
For I'm tired of you asking, did you cook? did you clean?

To obsess over housework does nothing for me
It's something I do, it does not define me.
Why should I have to be slave to a home?
The Lord gave me sense, and a mind of my own.

I want to discover with each passing day
The person I am, and where my interests lay
With eyes gently closed, and head humbly bowed
I pray to my Lord, someday you'd be proud.

Value in Christ

Don't base all your value in riches and wealth
Assuming you'll always be blessed with good health,
For relentless you labour to get what you can
In order to prove your success as a man.

When you have so much, and life seems a treat
And there's plenty of drink, and plenty to eat,
You can buy what you want, and you don't hesitate
And material gain is what makes you feel great.

What if, in an instant, all was taken away,
And you say your farewells to your once yesterday
When all faith in economy grinds to a halt
With nobody knowing just who is at fault.

Look to your future, rejoice and be glad,
Though you haven't as much as perhaps you once had.
You can have what is priceless, where security is found
For it's not in the dollar, and not in the pound.

For seeking the Lord is what you should do,
Since he is the answer to what you go through.
The greatest of things can you always afford
It's placing your value with Christ as your Lord.

He said that he'd always supply all our needs,
Not once did he promise to give us our greeds
There's only one way you can nourish your soul.
So make sure today, you let Christ take control.

Consider

Consider the old who live down your road,
Consider the burdened who carry their load,
Consider the poor who have nothing to eat,
Consider the runaway kids on the street.

Consider the addicts who live for their drugs,
Consider the man who was beaten by thugs,
Consider the diseases promiscuity breeds,
Consider the places disfunctionality leads.

Consider the knives, the guns and the crime,
Consider the prisoners doing their time,
Consider the people who are hurting inside -
Consider our world for which Jesus Christ died.

Getting Older

No longer the same, no longer a kid
And we may not function the way we once did.
The body is frail, the mind at times weak,
Remember the Lord is who we must seek.

When days turn to months, and months turn to years,
And we find we're still crying the very same tears,
The Lord, in his wisdom, knows what is best,
Whatever we go through, whatever our test.

For he knows our trials, and he knows our pain,
And trusting in him is no loss, only gain.
He'll answer our prayers, he is never too late,
For the answer will always be, Yes, No or Wait.

And life's full of twists, and many a turn,
No doubt there are lessons God wants us to learn.
He'll give us his strength, and carry us through
And direct our ways, so we know what to do.

Believe with your mind, accept with your heart
He was ready and waiting for you, right from the start.
So remember tonight, before you fall asleep
God's unfailing love, so priceless, so deep.

Positivity

Be positive whatever life may bring,
Think optimism for everything.
To let your problems weigh you down
Can only ever make you frown.

A cheerful heart works as a cure
For misery you must not endure.
Displace the bad, embrace the good -
Don't you think it's time you should?

Death

Looked deep into the bleak of night,
My spirit low and fist clenched tight -
The day that came, it now has gone,
But soon awaits another morn.

So it is like when death arrives,
And how it comes and shatters lives
Just like the closing of the day,
The rays of light they slip away.

But always look towards the dawn,
For when one dies another's born.
A new day that is fresh and bright
Awaits but yet another night.

In heaven there's eternal day
Where the light of life won't fade away
And pain and sorrow don't exist
Where death will surely not be missed.

A Winter's Night

Across the sky the wind doth blow,
The oh so stormy gusts of snow
Towards the hills, towards the street,
I wonder who it's going to meet.

A lady at the bus stop near
Is shivering at this time of year,
Her feet so cold, her fingers numb,
Just waiting for that bus to come.

The sun now dies beneath the hills,
And all along the window sills
I see the heaps of pure white snow
Portraying its beauty in a glistening glow.

The wind and snow finally cease,
And now returns the welcomed peace -
The quiet stillness of the night,
And I can sleep to my delight.

About the Author

The author Arlene Baptiste is the 3rd of 4 daughters born on the 12th May 1975. She was raised in the SDA church and is committed to her Christian faith. She has drawn strength from trusting God and believes in the great plans and purposes that He has for her own life. Over the years she has experienced God's supernatural strength and restoring power. She finds joy in expressing her thoughts through poetry and is passionate about her beliefs. By compiling this book, it is her desire that readers discover God for themselves and experience His unfailing love. She believes that though many times in our humanness we doubt God, we must remember that He can and will give us the strength to never give up on our hopes and dreams. God has the very best in store for all who believe in Him and call on his name, so continue praying and keep on believing!

Printed in Great Britain
by Amazon